Thoughts from both sides of the Rainbow

Thoughts from both sides of the Rainbow

poems and drawings
by Linda A. Pukalo

The Chapel Hill Press

© 1999 by Linda A. Pukalo

All Rights Reserved.
No portion of this book may be reproduced, by any process or technique, without the written consent of the publisher and copyright holder.

Linda A. Pukalo
Thoughts from both sides of the Rainbow/Linda A. Pukalo

Typesetting: Linda A. Pukalo & Jack Owens
Illustrations: Linda A. Pukalo
Cover Design: Geoff Reiss, Midgard Productions

Published by:
The Chapel Hill Press
100 Eastwood Lake Road
Chapel Hill, NC 27514
919/942-8389
Fax: 968-3274

www.chapelhillpress.com

Printed in The United States of America

ISBN: 1-880849-15-1

*For all your dreams
yet to be...
Is my wish to you from me...
With love,
Linda P.* ♥

To Laugh

To Cry

To Wonder Why

This book is dedicated
With Hope and
A Prayer and
A Wish and
A Dream
To God
And all my family and friends for standing by me in my darkest hour with their patience, strength and encouragement . . .
You know who you are . . .
May you Carry On
In Love, Light and Peace Always
Me

*In Loving Memory
of
Our Son
Anthony James
1989-1991
My Mother - Jessie
1926-1990
My Brother-in-Law - Bill
1946-1997
My Mother-in-Law - Sophia
1913-1999*

till we are together again . . .

TO

My son-Jason, My Husband-Jim
LeAnne, Jennifer
Andreas, Leah, Eddy
My Dad
My Brothers, Sister
In-Laws, Nieces, Nephews,
Aunts, Uncles, Cousins
Friends

Thank You

To all my friends along the path

who shared a tear and a laugh

For the thoughtful words you may have said

that somehow stuck inside my head

For helping me get through another day

For helping me be on my way

For helping me understand the price I paid

to be on this earth to love and play

To all of the authors whose books that I have read

for the words to the songs running through my head

God has helped me put the words into poems

Thoughts from everyone to be told!

CONTENTS

A Hope
Why
Thoughts from Both sides of the Rainbow
Wrinkles
The Dancing Light
What If
Wishes and . . .
A Gift
A Mother's Wish
An Angel Whispered
Essence
A Touch
Understand
A Princess
Why Did We Look Away
Blame it on the Weather
Dear Child
Which Way Do I Go?
I Just Need a Break
The Maze
Plaque On the Wall
Teen
My Dear Child
Unresolved Issues
I Wish
Make-up Mom & Me
Telephone
A Mother, A Princess, A King
Thinking of You
To My Friend
Time
Light
Together
Words
Rainbow Windows for Children

A Hope

I hope these poems are passed around
   they say nothing new or even profound
Just simple messages from me to you
      to inspire - when you are feeling blue
A collection of the poems that I wrote
      on the days, it was hard to function or cope
I hope they will inspire a different view
      of how you see . . . what happened to you
With Love,
   one lifetime,
      one day,
         one hour,
            one minute,
               one second,
                  one heartbeat at a time . . .

Why?

Why when you give a child a box of crayons
Do they draw a rainbow with their small hands?

How do they instinctively know
In what order the colors should go?

What is it they want to share
With the ones entrusted with their care?

What is it they want us to see
When they paint their rainbow for you and me?

Why I wrote
Thoughts from Both Sides of the Rainbow

Why did he have to die? I cannot tell you how many times I have asked myself that question.
Does any one have an answer?   I don't know.

I do know that we have to keep moving, for to give in to the despair that can so easily overcome you, can only serve to dishonor the memory of those we love, who have fought so hard to live. Because if you have taught someone to live and then when they die you forget how to live, than everything you taught them was a lie.

And they are such brave little fighters! Most of the children who are born with life-threatening illnesses have no clue what a normal life is like. They have taken medicine from day one, just to survive. I do know that they are the true angels on earth for they have such a beautiful light about them. They must be here to teach us so that we may have a better life for I do not think God intentionally creates the problems these little ones are faced with. I think the little ones chose to be born with whatever. They are on a mission of love to teach us whatever it is we need to know, to touch our lives and to leave the world a better place through all of those who have been touched by their special light.

When our son, AJ, died from a congenital heart defect at the age of two, eleven months after my mother died, from a brain tumor that took her life in two months, mine broke. In the process of trying to come to grips with what is now my reality, I have found many kind and caring individuals that I probably would have never met, otherwise.

In my search to try to make some sense out of life again or "Heal" as the politically correct may say - I have been blessed with the creative energies to envision a "Rainbow Tree or a Rainbow Window", to remember our loved ones as "Rainbows of Light" who bring us messages of hope during our darkest hours with the promise of the Rainbow.

I have been afforded the opportunity to have this vision come true, with a "Rainbow Window" on the fifth floor of Duke's Children's Hospital and a "Rainbow Star" in the pediatric intensive care unit at Wake Medical Center in Raleigh, NC. Presently, I continue to have this vision of a "Rainbow Window" in all Children's Hospitals . . . everywhere and anywhere that we need their message to remind us about the frailty of life, the beauty in life and their gentle prayer to appreciate the choices we have.

Also, during this search I have started to write poetry and have been encouraged by my "friends" to have them published. As you can see or read, I have taken their advice, so if you do not like this book you need to ask them for a refund. Just kidding!

I hope I have written a poem to touch your heart with a prayer that it may help to lighten your load, with wishes that you will find "Life is beautiful on both sides of the Rainbow"- and courage to follow your dreams!

Linda

Wrinkles

I look in the mirror and wonder when
    The lines and wrinkles became so etched in
I thought, "this cannot be my wrinkled skin,
    I do not feel that old within!"
I guess nature found a way to permanently trace
    Moments in time, by the wrinkles on my face
        Wrinkles I have earned over many years
        Wrinkles that trace the tracks of my tears
        Wrinkles from all of the disappointments of youth
        Wrinkles from those who were mean or uncouth
        Wrinkles from sadness, lost hope and disasters
        Wrinkles from the smiles of love and laughter
        Wrinkles from all the kisses I have shared
        Wrinkles from all of the dreams I have dared
        Wrinkles from all the lessons I have learned
        Wrinkles . . . every one of them . . . earned!
Now when I look in the mirror it is not wrinkles that I see,
    But the story of my life staring back at me!

The Dancing Light

The rainbow is an awesome sight
    An amazing display of dancing light
A symbol of God's, promise to us
    To believe in Him, with utmost trust
Many things happen, we don't understand
    But it is all part of our Creators plan
We spend precious time, trying to figure out why
    Our life has been changed, in the blink of an eye
Why do some of us live and some of us die?
    Are questions we ask with tears in our eyes

I have no answers to the questions you ask
    I'm just trying to see the light at the end of the path
My life has been changed by what has happened to me
    My Lord has opened my eyes and allowed me to see
His promise of Rainbows, an everlasting light
    And knowing I am never far, from His loving sight

The answers to questions, I had asked of Him
    Were all being answered, from somewhere within
I've found peace everywhere instead of despair
    In the beauty of life and in people who care
I saw God in all of us, somewhere inside
    Always trying to let us know, He is on our side
Always ready to help, if we give Him a chance
    "Dear Lord, please help me . . .
                        make it through this dance."

What has become one of my fears
      As I try to hold back all of the tears
           Is that if I ever let them go
                  Will I be able to stop the flow?

What IF?

What if in another time, another place
    We charted the course for the whole human race?

We all came together to decide who we would be
    We would make a difference if we could just be

And then we were born and our memories erased,
    Of what we would do when we arrived at this place

But, we managed to cover that very possibility
Because implanted in our memories, was some kind of key

A key that would somehow unlock and release
    The memories we had for world-wide peace

So be kind to those you happen to meet,
    For they may hold <u>the key</u> with the answers you seek!

Be kind to everyone for you never can tell,
    They may hold <u>the key</u> to free you from hell !

Wishes and . . .

Wishes and Hopes and Prayers and Dreams . . .
    How they turn out remains to be seen
You Wish upon a star at night
    Hoping everything will turn out right
        Praying hard with all your might
            Dear Lord, please help me see the light
Because the Dreams I had yesterday
        Are not the ones I have today . . .

A Gift

A light came down from the heavens above
    A precious gift conceived in love
A light to guide and lead the way
    To show us how to love and play
A light with special gifts to share
    To guide us with a gentle prayer
A light so bright with so much to give
    Sometimes dies, so that others may live

A Mother's Wish

Sometimes I laugh, Sometimes I cry
Trying to answer the question WHY

Why does a life that has just begun
    Have to miss out on so much fun?
Why this one? This child of mine,
    Why is he being cheated by father time?

You see your childhood was taken away,
    By the illness, they told us, you had, today.
From a little one who is barely two
    They are learning things they never knew.
A little one, just starting to live
    How much more can you be expected to give?

Now all we have is a hope and a prayer,
    And a wish that it was us, instead of you, lying there.
We have searched everywhere in hope of a cure.
But, Dear Lord, how much more, can our little one endure?

So, we hoped and we prayed and we asked for some time,
Time for some memories. Time for some fun.
Time just to be, with the ones that we love.

You never did make it to the age of three;
    But left in my dreams the thought of a tree.
A tree filled with rainbows, of hope, from above;
    A tree symbolizing life, rainbows of hope, and of love.

Our children are special in so many ways
And this is how I will remember them for all of my days;
Little "Rainbows of Light" shinning brightly everywhere!
Helping us through, all of life's despairs,
    By bringing us hope . . . and a wish . . . and a prayer . . .

Make a wish if you dare; make a wish two or three,
But first make a wish for all yet to be . . .

In Loving Memory of our Son, A.J.
    and of all children whose dreams are yet to be

An Angel Whispered in My Ear

One day an angel whispered in my ear, about the life you led,
She saw a special child, who spends too much time in bed.

She told me of the injustices, that you must endure,
Because they're trying very hard, to find that special cure.
A cure that will let you run and play, like other children do.
A cure that will let you see and be, the age of ninety-two.

She also saw a family, ripped and torn apart,
By their loved ones illness, that is tearing at their heart.
They are trying hard to smile, in the midst of all their fears,
But they're overcome with sadness, and can't hold back the tears.

She heard them pray for just a day, a lovely memory.
A day where you'd be playing, as happy as can be.
A day of something special, to take away the tears.
A day that they could cherish, in the coming years.

"Dear Lord," I heard her whisper, "isn't there something you can do?
This family seems to be fast slipping, from your special view.
This family needs to smile again, forgetting all this grief,
Won't you please make an exception, and give them some relief?"

"Look around my little angel and I'll tell you what I see
Because there are angels everywhere, taking up for me!

They are standing by this bedside, all dressed up in white,
Trying everything they know, to help you through the night.
Although they have no answers, to the question why,
They always have a shoulder, to rest your head and cry.

Over there I see your family, standing with your friends,
They're trying very hard, but can't seem to comprehend,
You see they seem so helpless, 'cause there's not much they can do,
Still they're on a mission: they hope and pray for you.

Now, someone's looking over at you, and looking up at me,
I think he heard your whispers, I think he heard your plea.
I think he heard about that child, the one with special needs,
I think all of your prayers have sowed, a very magical seed."

And then I heard a whisper, from the one who heard your prayer.
"we'll have to find the bright side, through all of this despair
this child leads a life down here, that isn't very fair.
We'll have to show him, Lord, that the people here do care!

Dear Lord, I think there's something, that's in our power to do.
We'll grant a wish for every one, and then we'll see it through.
With the help of special friends down here,
                                       and the support we get from you,
You know we'll move the heavens, to make that wish come true."

"And so my little angel, look around and you will see
Those faces looking back at you . . . are taking up for me."

Essence

One of the many things I have buried inside
    Is the essence of me – I try to hide
The essence of what is really me
    And not of what you want me to be
The essence that I am afraid to show
    For then my friends will truly know
How I have stunted my efforts to love and grow
    To hide the truth with an elaborate show

But I must say in my own defense
    Of this elaborate, misguided pretense
I was hiding my essence from you -- you see
    Because I was afraid, you wouldn't understand me

But now I know what matters most
    And to this, I offer a loving toast
"To the angel hiding deep inside
    Spread your wings – it's time to fly!"

A Touch

A peck on the cheek, a half-hearted hug
    is the touch we get from the ones that we love
It's become the fashionable touch of hello and good-bye
    and even when someone has tears in their eyes
No wonder we are grumpy and say we are stressed
    we have forgotten the value of a loving caress
Maybe much of the stress would be relieved every day
    if all of us hugged and kissed the old-fashioned way
Our day would start with a warm and loving embrace
    and end with a kiss on the lips of your face
Just think how much better all of us would feel
    like when mom gave us a kiss and said we were healed
So maybe if we took an extra minute or two
    with the ones who we pledged our life with "I do"
To start every day with a warm and loving embrace
    There would be memories of kisses . . .
              instead of stress on our face!

Doesn't everyone in the world
have family and friends
      They want to grow old with
            so they can "remember when"?

Understand

"I am not going to try and understand anymore"
    Is the sign I am posting on my front door
I am tired of trying to understand
    The follies of my fellow man
Why can't they seem to understand
    The destruction and hurt they have caused to our great land.
Do they honestly think the harm that they do
    Will not affect them – only me and you?
I know many have tried to change their point of view
    But what will it take for the message to get through?
Many groups have formed to turn things around
They enlighten and shock us with the facts that they've found
Some listen intently, some don't even blink
    When they tell us a plant or an animal is extinct!
We are tired of the messes, we don't want anymore
    Polluting our waters and spoiling our shores
Killing the seafood on which we depend
    Please tell me - What has to happen – How will it end?

A loving touch, a warm embrace
Would help this world be a better place

A friendly word, a smiling face
Would bring together the human race

A Princess

A Princess is gone, forever interred
   What have we learned?

She has given us gifts; she has sown many seeds
   do you think we can carry on with her good deeds?
Do you think instead of wasting energy trying to figure out why
   we could continue the work started by *a Princess* who died?
If we each took a charity and fulfilled one of its needs
   wouldn't that be the best legacy indeed?

She openly shared her life for all to see
   inside the heart of royalty
She had shown she was not very different from us all
   she had problems like the rest of us, some big and some small
She endured the media's relentless pursuit
   she had little privacy and her deeds they'd dispute
It takes courage to live a life on display
   still her light touched many of us in a special way

     a light that shone brightly for such a short while
     a light that enjoyed a hug and a smile
     a light that helped when there was a need
     a light that hoped we follow her lead

No one is perfect we can just do our best
   to help where we can amid the unrest
We all have the light somewhere within
   so believe with your heart and the healing begin
And together we can lift our spirits High
   so never again will we say good-bye

Now all I can say, if nothing was learned
   A Princess is gone, forever interred

In Loving Memory of Princess Di & Mother Theresa
1997 ©

Sometimes the smiles
       On the faces that you see
           Are masking a pain
                Too deep . . . to be seen

Why Did We Look Away?

To say I know what you are going through
    Would be a lie and unfair to you.
Incestuous acts hidden from view
    took your innocence away from you,
A precious child was lost, on that fateful day
    Because heads had turned and looked away
A beautiful person you turned out to be
    Despite all of those haunting memories,
"Protecting the children" became your crusade
    fueled by the memories that never would fade.

Now something has happened I can see it in your eyes
    And I'm not sure if this time you are going to survive
I love you my friend and now it's our turn
    To take care of you with all that we've learned
You have taught all of us, from your own private hell
    That we could survive, anything, and still turn out well
The anger you have kept hidden from view
    is making you think no one could really love you
But that is where you are making a mistake
    We love you, believe in you and will do what ever it takes.

You do not think you can trust anyone - anymore
Because you have been let down, so very, many times before
Please listen to me and don't run anymore
    Your children need the mother, they love and adore
It is time to let go, of those feelings inside
    I promise to help you, I'll be by your side
But until you can admit that you need some help
    It is too painful for me to watch, as you destroy yourself

This time no one is looking away
    And we grieve for the child that was lost on that day
We pray and we hope you will seek some help
    And feel that you can not handle this all by yourself
You are smart and intelligent and I hope you recognize
    The path you have chosen is not very wise
You are a beautiful woman, we all admire and adore
    You have all of the keys, why won't you open the door?

Why is it when
     your life's in a mess
          It's hard to remember
               how much you are blessed?

Blame It On The Weather

Every day you seem to hear someone complain
    of the heat, the cold, the wind or the rain

No one is ever very satisfied
    with the weather that is going on outside

Maybe it is a reflection of what is going on inside
    a grief they may feel from someone who died
    of feelings that no one will acknowledge anymore
    leaving them feeling alone and ignored

It's too hot, it's too cold, it's too windy, it's too wet
    seems to be . . . a never-ending lament
    words that are spoken and not really meant
    words that are spoken with sympathy as their intent

They can complain about the weather, someone will listen to them
    it is safe and non-threatening and will not offend

The weather is here so you don't have to pretend
    your heart is still broken – not ready to mend

The weather is here so when you feel lousy inside
    from the pain that gets harder and harder to hide
    you can say you feel lousy . . .because it's nasty outside
    and then there is no further need to explain

So think of this verse next time you hear someone complain
    of the heat, the cold, the wind or the rain
    for when we can no longer deal with the pain

God gives us bad weather as something to blame
    and He gives us . . . tomorrow . . . a brand new day!

There is a label we all share
It's on clothes that we all wear

Handle with Care

Dear Child

I know that you are feeling scared and confused
And worried about what is going to happen to you
God is there in your heart, listening through all of your tears
Waiting for you to ask him, to take away your fears.
What is happening between your mom and your dad
Is NOT your fault, it is very, very sad

I want you to know, we are all praying for you,
And all of the things, that you are going through.
We are not taking sides, between your mom and your dad
we're not supposed to judge, who's good and who's bad.
Only your parents and God, know what is true
We love them and pray for them, so they can be there for you.
Pray that they ask God, to help them find their way
So you can just be a child, with no worries, but play!
I hope that these words, help you to feel better
But I wish I could hug you, instead of, sending this letter.
We love you and you are in our prayers

Everyone is where they are supposed to be
Sharing their talents with you and me

Which Way do I Go?

Which path do I take? Which way do I go?
What choices do I make . . .and how will I know . .
If the steps I am taking will help me to grow?
I can only believe that whatever path I may take
Is right for me and not a mistake.
That if choices are made with love and light
I will always be guided to a new height.
And if, at every step and every turn
Brings something new for me to learn.
Then I guess I really do not need to ask
If I am on . . . the right path.

I Just Need A Break

Today I don't want to go anywhere
I just want to sit in my favorite chair
I just want to put my feet up someplace
    And just take a break from the routine and pace
I don't even care if they smell or they stink
I just want to sit here and not even think!
I don't want the remote – take the phone off the hook
    And don't even think of asking me to cook!
I have had all the running around I can take
    Forgive me my family – I just need a break!

I just need a break from all the driving around
    Every day back and forth all across town
Looking for things, we think that we need
    Buying some things, we really don't need

There is someplace to go every night of the week
    and the thought of the pace leaves me feeling weak
There is soccer and scouts and groceries to get
    and I haven't even started thinking about dinner yet!
In between that – there is piano and ballet
    and NO there isn't any time to go out and play!
Cook dinner, clean up, take a bath and to bed
    What is this pounding inside of my head?

It's ten o'clock and I have no energy left for you
    Have I told you lately – How Much I Love You?

People drawn together
  from where they've been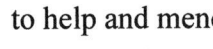
     Hearts drawn close
        to help and mend

The Maze

Life is like a complicated maze
    For you to travel all of your days
Some paths will lead you to a dead end
    And some paths will make you start over again
But the right path will possess many twists and turns
    Special opportunities for you to flourish and learn
On some paths you may meet a new friend
On some paths you may see a relationship end
On some paths you may leave an old friend behind
    Because they are some other place . . . at this moment in time
And then at some point you may meet again
    To be joined on the path, with your dear old friend
Remembering together that life's circumstance
    Has brought you together to learn a new dance
Remembering together that life's just a never-ending quest
    To be loving and kind and to just do your best!
Remembering together the different choices you faced
    And laughing together now . . . that you're at the same place!

Listen to those thoughts deep within
They will always guide and be your friend
They will never let you go astray
They will always help you make it . . .
                           through the day!

The Plaque On The Wall

I picked up a plaque one day at the mall
And gave it to mom for no reason at all
She smiled and tacked it up on the wall

I know I pointed to it, once or twice through the years
When my parents and I argued to the point of tears
Because I could not understand all of their fears

I heard the smile in my dad's voice as he read it to me
And now I think, I understand what he used to mean
Because now, I am the parent of one of those teens

I still think that plaque is a pretty useful tool
when everyone is arguing and confusion's the rule
Just point to the plaque and say with a laugh
"Help me Dear Lord so that this too may pass"

So just for the record and all purposes and intent
I hope I can say what I mean and mean what I meant
I'll quote it to you because that's only right
The author is unknown but it's marked copyright!

"I know you believe you understand what you think I said but I am not sure you realize that what you heard is not what I meant" ©

Words of wisdom from *The Plaque On The Wall*

Teen

I remember back when I was a teen
      And thought my parents were too strict and mean
    I thought that they never listened to me
I thought that they were stifling me
Because all I wanted was for them to love and understand me

So I began to test their love over and over again
      when I started to bring home some of my friends
I tested them with – the clothes I would wear
I tested them with – the style of my hair
I tested them with things – I knew that were dumb
I tested them even – when it wasn't very fun
I tested their patience and their love for me
Because all I wanted was for them to love and understand me
      And now, I am the parent of that very same teen!

Why can't we accept someone doing his or her best
    Let everything go - and just give it a rest
Just accept all the good they have set out to do
    And leave the judgement of their character . . .
                          To a higher review

My Dear Child

The time has come to let you go
So you can test your wings as you continue to grow
I don't know what paths or roads you will take
Trying times will be many and you may make mistakes
But you will be growing and learning to master your fate

I vow not to control or impose my point of view
I promise to state my concerns and leave decisions to you
I will not be tolerant of drugs or abuse
I love you too much so you'll have to choose
But I will always be there as someone you can trust
To count on or lean on, any time you must
I can hold your hand and listen to you
And hope that my love will guide you through
I do not profess to know all the mysteries of earth
I'm glad you are the one to whom I gave birth
I am awed by the thought God gave you to me
And I have the pleasure of . . . just watching you be

With Love Forever and Always
Mom & Dad

When you open your mind,
    you get a much better view
        Of who people are
            and what they mean to you

Unresolved Issues

I cleaned my mother-in-laws home out today
    Lord, help me get through this I heard myself pray
I have unresolved issues to take up with you
    Couldn't you have stayed another year maybe two?
You were independent and stubborn, didn't need any help
    When asked, you'd always say "I'll do it myself"
I just wanted a chance "to repay" if you must
    All of the things that you have done for us
Now we sit here surrounded by all of "your stuff"
    trying to choose what to keep . . . can really be tough
It's hard to know what all these memories meant
    So all I can do is sit here and vent!
Asking you why you didn't write a line or two
    To share why "this stuff" was so special to you
I know there is a story behind everything in this room
    But the stories are gone now, they're locked in the tomb
Why didn't you write a little note maybe two
    To share with those, now mourning for you
A special note for everyone left behind
    Remembering a special moment . . .
                      from your past and mine

I Wish....

Once I had an awesome wish
That everything could be fixed with a hug and a kiss
I wished with all my strength and might
But my kisses just couldn't make it right
And now I put my faith in you
And hope that you will see it through
Because I still have that awesome wish
That everything could be fixed with a hug and a kiss

Do You?

Make - Up, Mom & Me

She would wake up in the morning and *"put on her face"*
   I guess this was mom's way of coping with the never-ending pace
Then she would make coffee and toast for my dad
   Even if she was feeling bad, angry, or sad
Then, there was the four of us, she got on their way
   Then straightened the house, because she worked every day

Again in the afternoon I would see her *"put on her face"*
   I would ask *"Mom why do you put make-up on your face?"*
She would tell me it was "to look good for your dad,
   Who wants to come home, to someone who looks bad?"
She would tell me it was because when she was feeling sick
   At least, looking in the mirror wouldn't make her go "ick!"
She would tell me that whenever going someplace
   People would much rather look . . . at a pretty face!

A simple philosophy, so wise and so true
       Her special way of saying, I Love You

Now I wake up in the morning and *"put on my face"*
   And try to make sense of the never-ending pace
And there's rarely an occasion I go any place
   Without putting some make-up, on my face

There is shopping and working and things I must do
   All while I think and care about you
And now my son asks me *"why, that I must*
   Put on some make-up if we're in such a rush?"

Should I tell him I wear it because it is kind of a shield
   between how I look and how I feel?
Should I tell him I wear it because people smile instead
   of asking you what is going on in your head?
Should I tell him I wear it to hide the tears that I cry
   because I am missing the brother, he had , who died?
Should I tell him I wear it because I have almost given up hope
   and I don't know how I am going to cope?

   And I hear myself tell him "whenever going someplace
   People would much rather look . . . at a well-groomed face!"

And then I was somewhere just the other day
   And someone told me I looked pretty today!
I said "Thank you" as I turned, my head away
   Because all of my make-up was washing away
And then I heard someone whisper
   "Go dry your eyes and go fix your face
   I'm just saying I Love You from some other place"

Thank God for make-up is all I can say
   Because make-up does wonders on some of those days
               June 1997

The Telephone

I remember when I could pick up the phone
    From anywhere I was I could call home
And there you would be on the end of the line
    Saying "hello – yes everything is fine."
I could listen to your voice and hear you smile
    Even though we were separated by so many miles
Even though we sent cards and also wrote letters
    I still liked the sound of your voice . . . so much better
Your voice was transported through time and space
    To comfort me in some far away place
We would talk for hours about anything at all
    And many times forgot the purpose of the call
Just hearing your voice on the other end of the line
        Transcending space . . .
                Transcending time . . .

Then you would say, *"that's enough for today*
    or the phone company's going to get all of your pay!"
"I can't hear your voice when you're dead and gone
    so it really doesn't matter that we've talked for so long
And I'm not ready to get off the telephone – just yet
    you know there are no phone lines - to heaven yet!"
Then you would say with a laugh *"imagine that!"*
    and we would continue on with our chat
Now there are so many days there isn't anything I wouldn't do
    If I could just pick up the phone and talk to you . . .
Just to hear your voice on the other end of the line
        Transcending space . . .
                Transcending time . . .

Black and white and shades of gray
We always want others to see it our way

Black or white or red or green
Why is someone's color or belief
                        a reason to be mean?

A Mother, A Princess, A King

A Mother looked after those who lived in poverty
A Princess had it all – she was royalty
A King had a dream of equality
What does it mean?

A mother looked after the sick and the poor
She saw hope in the eyes of the ones we ignored
She treated everyone she met with dignity and respect
She changed many lives by the example she set
She spent a lifetime working quietly to fulfill her dream
Trying to teach others . . . what life really means

A Princess had it all – she was royalty
Still she lived a life full of reality
She gave the gift of herself to many charities
And let the whole world see all of her frailties

Some candles burn long, some candles burn bright
And a King had many when he marched in the night
Proclaiming quite loudly that he had a dream
Never quite understanding, those who were vicious and mean

What is wrong with us that we cannot trust
The ones who have the guts and the dreams to help us?
They give of themselves – they ask for nothing in return
They just want to be – and share what they have learned
If all of us are human - we all have a past
Why is humanity out of our grasp?

A Mother looked after those who lived in poverty
A Princess had it all – she was royalty
A King had a dream of equality
All are now victims of reality

In Memory of Mother Theresa, Princess Di, & M L King Jr

Thinking of You

You often sent cards, out of the blue
The one's that said "I'm thinking of You"
I don't think I told you how much that they meant
I hope you never wondered if the postage was well spent
With thoughts and messages to brighten and cheer
It seemed like those cards would magically appear
I wondered if you knew in some mystical way
That you answered a prayer - that I had - on that day
Now I just want to tell you, out of the blue
My thoughts and my prayers
are <u>always</u> with
<u>*You*</u>

To My Friend

I hope that I've told time and a again
    How much it has meant to be considered your friend
I hope that I've told you - you've opened my eyes
    With words that were gentle,
            sometimes cruel, but so wise
I hope that I've told you that your inspiration
    Gave new meaning to the words:
            strength and determination

I hope that I've told you how much it has meant
    Just being a friend and allowing me to vent
    To feel safe enough and comfortable to confide
        Those innermost feelings we sometimes hide
    To never have judged the things I would say or do
        Are the attributes I admired most in you
I hope that I've told you
    what a wonderful world this would be
If every one could be a friend like you are/were to me
    In Love, Light and Friendship Always

Who would have thought – ten years ago
We were all in our prime and raring to go

Who would have thought - all the joy and the fun
Would come down to the memory of belonging to one

Who would have thought – it would come down to this
To the tears on my face as I give you one last kiss

Who would have thought - when it's all said and done
The question I would have was "did you have fun?"

Time

Time does not stand still my friend
    Not for you, me or the wind
Time just keeps on ticking by
    Not even pausing to ask why?
Even on the day you died—
    Time just kept on ticking by
Even as my world came to an end
    Time did not stand still -- even then

There was a time I thought it should
There was a time I thought it would
There was a time I thought it ceased
    when I was searching for some peace
When all that I held near and dear
    Time just seemed to disappear

Once when time was my friend
    we thought that time would never end
But that was in another time and place
    when I could gaze upon and touch your face
There is one thing time cannot do
    that is take away . . . the memory of you
Time can never, never erase
    the memories you left . . . in time . . .in space
        or the memories of your kisses . . . on my face

Maybe one day
    we won't have to die
        We'll just open our hearts
            and together we'll fly

Light

Sometime during life's darkest hour
    I saw a light with awesome power
A light so beautiful and so surreal
A light to comfort and help me heal
A light so pure it let me see
    The place you were going when you left me
A light so glorious it humbled me
    When the Lord came here to set you free!

No one can begin to know your feelings
Or how many endless hours, you stare up at ceilings
While some illness is relentlessly stealing
And drugs have left you weak and reeling
As you contemplate the reason why
One as young as you . . . may die

Together

Once, when we were very young
    there were so many songs, to be sung
So many things, exciting and new
    a brand new world to share with you!

But time was not on our side
    and many things changed, the day you died.
There is a sadness now I carry inside
    with all of the tears, I have to hide.

Now I spend my time thinking of you
    and all the things we had a chance to do.
The tears and sadness are still there
    but, now I see you everywhere
    like a scent that lingers in the morning air.

And given the beauty of each new birth
    Come to bless us all, here on earth
An awesome lesson I have learned from you
    That life goes on . . . it does renew

I love you now, I loved you then,
    And now I know, I'll love you when
        We are back together . . . again . . .

Words

As I write the words just seem to flow
       From where they come I do not know
I'd like to think they are written with love
I'd like to think I'm guided from above
I'd like to think they inspire hope
I'd like to think they're kind of a rope
I'd like to think they'll pull you through
       When something bad happens to you
I'd like to think they are wise and kind
I'd like to think they'll stand the test of time
But most of all I'd like to think
       These words are written with indelible ink
And I hope my words won't fade away
       Like my dreams for you did . . . yesterday

In Loving Memory

Rainbow Originals would love to create more "Rainbow Windows for Children" & <u>*You*</u> *have helped*

Give Someone you LOVE
   Wishes of Hope and the Promise of the Rainbow

A Keepsake designed to encompass the spirituality of life

The metal represents life . . . a constant
The glass represents the frailty of life
The rainbows, reflected by the sunlight on the glass,
Represent all who have hopes and dreams . . .
And life's imperfections are mirrored by the imperfection
in my work . . . which reflects the true beauty of life

Rainbow Originals came about after our son died from a congenital heart defect, and a "seed" was planted in my dreams . . . I wanted to bring smiles and hope into the lives of the children in hospitals by creating *"Rainbow Windows"*. These magical windows use moving crystals and glass to create rainbows across a hospital wing to delight and inspire those who may be there for months. If they cannot go out perhaps a small piece of the outside can come in, bringing the light, love and hope with it.

I know what this can mean for children and their families through personal experience with our son A.J. In 1994, I was afforded the opportunity to put one of my "living" "Rainbow Windows" on the fifth floor in Duke Children's Hospital. Then again in 1997, I had the privilege of putting a "Rainbow Star" in the atrium of the pediatric intensive care unit at Wake Medical Center in Raleigh, NC.

Today, I still have the dream that all children share this beautiful gift; inspired by the life and death of our son, as I continue to engrave Commemorative Crystals that celebrate the milestones in life.

Grief has become A Rainbow, A Dream, and A Vision. A visual statement of how the beauty of the soul lives on in light and love by the sunlight shining through the crystal creating a rainbow, with a message of hope from them to us about the frailty of life, the beauty of life that surrounds us, and our choices in life, as we pursue our dreams.

By purchasing this book or ordering a crystal YOU are helping this "seed" grow into a beautiful and unique forest as a tribute to our loved ones whose lives are cut short, leaving their dreams yet to be . . . And for this I thank you, for giving this mother an opportunity to make life a little brighter, by bringing wishes of hope and the promise of the rainbow to a child and their family.

With Hope and A Prayer and A Wish and A Dream

In Conclusion

The following notes are just three of many that I have received. They express what I envisioned and hoped the "Rainbow Window and Crystals" would mean to others who are on the on the same path, and they comfort me because I feel that they are also spiritual messages from my son – letting me know "I'm fine, now—mom-Carry on. . ."

A Volunteer Writes:

"As a Make-A-Wish volunteer and wish granter, I want to tell you how much I enjoy my glass creations I received at the 1997 and 1998 Volunteer Recognition Dinners. They hang in my kitchen window and remind me of the children, their families, and other volunteers I have met during my time with this organization.

I also want to tell you how much I appreciate your commitment to making a personalized crystal for each wish child. When I follow up with the families I've worked with, they often mention how much the gift means to them.

I visited a family in the hospital recently whose child underwent a bone marrow transplant shortly after his wish for a computer was granted. One of the first things the mother did was express her gratitude for the beautiful glass she received in the mail with her sons name and wish date etched on it. Your creations are treasured immensely by these families! Truly," A.P.

A Parent Writes:

"Sept 5th 1996, my daughter was diagnosed with an inoperable brain stem tumor at the age of 22 months. We weren't given much hope, but took her to Duke Children's Hospital for chemotherapy. I can't tell you how many times I went and looked at the Rainbow Window you made for the childrens wing up there. It was such a beautiful light in such a dark time. . .I have felt ready to break this week from all of the pressure and when I opened that box and saw the beautiful glass, all the frustration and sadness inside me bubbled out. It reminded me that I am not alone and others have walked this road before me . . .I thank you for being a candle in the dark to our family at this tough time." JF

A Child Writes:

Dear Mrs Pukalo

You may not know me but I am one of the kids you sent a "Memory Rainbow Crystal." I just wrote to say thank you for the wonderful gift. I'm very sorry for what happened to your son. I think you are a talented mother to have created something so pretty. I just want to say thank you again. Well I have to go. Bye. Love T.J.

If you have any ideas or information on how to accomplish this vision, or if you would like to sponsor a "Rainbow Window/Tree" in a hospital or some other public place, please contact Linda at:

Rainbow Originals

Linda A Pukalo
www.rainbows4you.com lpukalo@earthlink.net
919-559-7912